Poetry Study

Songs of Ourselves
Volume 1, Part 3

CIE IGCSE Literature in English 0475 and 0992 for examination in 2020 and 2021

Contents

Widows Mull
The Tower
Thank you man
Mrs Manould

Introduction

This guide is intended to support students working towards CIE 0475 and 0992. As you know, poetry can be interpreted in different ways, so what I am offering here are some thoughts – absolutely NOT the last word on these poems. Your teacher will introduce you to the poems in a variety of different ways, but it isn't always easy to make all the notes you would like to in class. This guide is back-up. It doesn't tell you how to answer exam questions, although towards the end there are a few hints and some exam-style questions to consider. The most important thing is that you get to know the poems well. If you know a poem, you develop a feeling for it and your response will be much more original and heartfelt. Your teacher will ensure you have the exam practice you need. Italicised technical terms are explained in the Glossary at the end of the book.

Good luck - and enjoy these fantastic poems.

Jane Chumbley

Caged Bird - Maya Angelou

On a simple level this poem is about two birds - one is free and one is caged. The experience of the two birds is contrasted with marked shifts in tone (see Voice and Tone below). The free bird is joyful, and content; the caged bird is frustrated and angry. The birds are almost certainly being used, however, to represent human experience and, in particular, the experience of racial oppression in the United States. The free bird can be seen to represent the white American experience of freedom, ownership, luxury and privilege, whilst the caged bird reflects the frustrating restriction and desperation of the black African-American experience - both the slave culture and the racial segregation and prejudice which followed. Ironically, however, it is not the free bird who sings. By giving the song to the caged bird Angelou is arguably looking to inspire future generations - both black and white - to use their voice, to keep dreaming and to celebrate freedom where it is experienced.

Form and Structure

The poem is structured around contrast and alternating stanzas about the two birds, with stanzas 3 and 6 imposed as a repeated refrain. This at once highlights the contrast in the experience of the two birds with the word 'But' used twice - at the start of stanzas 2 and 5 - as a structural pivot. You could argue that Angelou reflects the privilege of the free bird by giving it first place in the poem. What's interesting, though, is the fact that the caged bird is the one which sings and the one which has the last word. The repetition of the refrain stanza and the final lines of stanzas 2 and 5 from 'his wings are clipped' suggests a determination: because the caged bird cannot fly, its voice is the only means it has to express its individuality and so 'he opens his throat to sing'. In the end, of course, the poem is about the 'Caged Bird' of the title - the free bird is just there to show the contrast.

The poem has no formal pattern in terms of line/stanza length or rhyme scheme but the poet generates a lot of rhythm and pace through sporadic (occasional) rhyme and verb patterns (see Language).

Voice and Tone
The poetic voice is that of a third person omniscient narrator. The tone varies sharply when the different birds are described, in order to highlight the contrast. Stanza 1 is joyful, energetic, almost exuberant as the bird 'leaps' and 'floats' and 'dips' and 'dares'. Stanza 2 is dark and ominous as the bird 'stalks' and can 'seldom see' in a 'narrow' cage with 'bars of rage'. He is 'clipped' and 'tied'. Similarly the tone of Stanza 4 is gentle and peaceful as the free bird 'thinks', the fat worms are 'waiting' and the 'breeze' is 'soft' in the 'sighing trees'. By contrast Stanza 5 is almost gothic in its horror with a deathly 'grave of dreams', 'shouts' and 'a nightmare scream'.

Language
The images of the natural world are strong in the stanzas of the free bird but also, interestingly, in the refrain about the caged bird. There is a light, bright positivity about 'the orange sun's rays' and the 'dawn-bright lawn'. The wind is personified as the free bird leaps 'on the back of the wind', while a similar effect is seen when the trees are 'sighing'. Angelou uses sibilance here: the repeated 's' sounds of 'trade winds soft through the sighing trees' create *onomatopoeia* - we can hear the whispering of the leaves. There's also a sense of *personification* with the almost comic image of the 'fat worms waiting on a dawn-bright lawn' - a ready meal offering itself up for the free bird. All this, and the fact that the free bird

'dares to claim the sky' and 'names the sky his own' really emphasises how nature serves the privileged free bird. Angelou is arguably using these initially very positive images to suggest something much darker about white privilege and colonisation - the way people have historically claimed ownership of a land or territory which was not their own. The fact that the adjective 'fat' is used to describe the worms suggests luxury and indulgence. The 'trade winds' may be a subtle reference to the Middle Passage - the route used by the slave ships.

But the caged bird's song is 'heard/on the distant hill'. The image of nature here is not decorated, it is much simpler: the hill is far away but the song is having an impact. This is an image of hope and inspiration.

The verbs in the first two stanzas create two opposing *lexical fields* - of freedom and captivity. Contrast 'leaps', 'floats', 'dips' and 'dares' with 'stalks', 'clipped' and 'tied'. These verbs tell a story of alienation: there is something fundamentally wrong when a bird cannot move freely in the way he should. But also notice, crucially, that the caged bird 'opens' his throat: this is the only way he can express himself.

Although there is no formal rhyme scheme the rhyme of 'trill', 'still' and 'hill' is very strong in the refrain - again emphasising the power of the caged bird's voice, even if it is a '**fearful** trill', an adjective that highlights the *paradox* of this singing - it is powerful but ominous because the bird sings of a freedom it can only imagine from captivity.

Metaphor is used elsewhere, not just in the *personification* of nature. The cage, for example, can be seen as a metaphor for racism, while the 'bars of rage' are a metaphor for frustration. When the caged bird's 'shadow shouts', the *alliteration* brings emphasis to a metaphor for frustration and futility - how can a shadow shout? It seems pointless, but the bird persists.

Themes
- Freedom and captivity
- Voice
- Isolation
- Determination
- Hope

Did You Know?
Angelou, a black civil rights activist, probably based her poem and the title of her autobiography - *I Know Why the Caged Bird Sings* - on the poem *Sympathy* by another American poet Paul Laurence Dunbar. Angelou was reportedly mute for six years following a traumatic experience so had, perhaps, a strong interest in the idea of finding a voice.

Prompt Questions
- What similarities can you see between Angelou's poem and *Sympathy* by Paul Laurence Dunbar?
- Is this a poem about animal cruelty?
- What does it mean that the free bird does not sing?
- Why has Angelou used the gendered pronoun 'he' for both birds?
- Is this poem political or personal?

Sonnet 43 - Elizabeth Barrett Browning
This is one of the older poems in your collection. Published in 1850, it is one of a series of *Sonnets from the Portuguese* written by

Victorian poet Elizabeth Barrett Browning for her future husband, Robert Browning (also a poet). The Little Portuguese was his pet name for her.

The first line introduces the poem's content and it's as if she is responding to a question he has asked: 'How do I love thee? Let me count the ways!' with the exclamation mark conveying something of her excitement at this listing project. She goes on to describe very methodically about eight or nine different ways she loves him, presenting a clear picture of an incredibly intense almost spiritual love which is absorbing every part of her life. The poem is *hyperbolic* in the way she commits every part of herself to him but there is something charming and almost naive about this which has made it an extremely popular poem for over 150 years.

The love she describes is completely unselfish, pure, eternal, idealised and powerfully transformative. It has healed her 'old griefs' and restored a love she thought she had lost for ever. She uses so much religious language that it's almost as if her love for Browning is a kind of religion to her. He has saved her. However, Barrett Browning doesn't reject Christian faith - in fact she says she will love Browning after death 'if God choose', implying that she still believes. The different ideas about the nature of her love are pulled out in detail below (see Language).

Form and Structure

The poem is a traditional sonnet in that it has 14 lines and a regular rhyme scheme with only four rhymes (abbaabbacdcdcd) - no mean feat in English! Each line is an *iambic pentameter* - diDUM diDUM diDUM diDUM diDUM - which is the rhythm of normal speech. So the poem sounds very natural, particularly when she introduces *caesurae* towards the end of the poem to inject some breathless passion and even more excitement.

The first eight lines - *the octet* - introduce a series of ways 'I love thee'. The remaining six lines - *the sestet* - develop the sense that she loves him with all the love she has ever had or will have - from childhood until after death.

The dominant structural feature of the poem is repetition, with the phrase 'I love thee' used nine times. Six lines begin with this phrase - a technique called *anaphora*. Anaphora or anaphoric repetition is a device used to create really strong emphasis and a sense of urgent enthusiasm or determination. It also puts a lot of stress on the words that follow such as the parallel adverbs *freely/purely*.

Voice and Tone

The poem is written in the first person and we know that it is autobiographical so we can refer to the speaker as 'she'. She uses direct address when she says 'thee' and although we know she was writing to Browning, it can seem as though the reader is being addressed directly.

Language

I love thee....

- 'to the depth and breadth and height/My soul can reach': the triple, *syndetic list* and religious language make this feel hyperbolic. She's indicating the scale of her love - it's actually immeasurable, beyond anything tangible.
- 'to the level of every day's/Most quiet need': this is juxtaposed to the previous image in that it is very domestic, ordinary and everyday. She loves him calmly and constantly.

- 'by sun and candlelight': these are symbols of day and night but also of life and hope. She loves him 24/7.
- 'freely, as men strive for Right': the capitalisation here and with *Being/Grace/Praise* highlights words which create a *lexical field* of religion. It is this which creates the idea her love is like a kind of religion to her. She loves him in an unconstrained, unforced, natural, honourable and good way. It is effortless to her. It also implies she will fight for him because it is the right or moral thing to do.
- 'purely, as they turn from Praise': this is a parallel phrase to the one above, with *alliteration* to link the adverb 'purely' into the capitalised lexical set. She loves him in a modest, virtuous way, without any hope of reward.
- 'with the passion put to use/In my old griefs': the *enjambment* here creates pace, suggesting her excitement. She has converted all the passion of her grief into a romantic passion. In this way her love can be seen as transformative.
- 'with my childhood's faith': again we see that religious language and get a sense that she loves him in an open, innocent, spiritual way. In some ways, he's like a god to her.
- 'with a love I seemed to lose/With my lost saints': it's likely she is referring here to dead relatives, but again we get the sense that her love for him brings hope and new life.
- 'with the breath/Smiles, tears, of all my life!: this is where she really winds up the energy. The list of three is now *asyndetic* - without the ands which slow a list down and make it ponderous. The *enjambment* adds to the effect of her enthusiasm spilling over the line. Everything she has - the complete range of her emotions - is poured into her love for him.
- 'better after death': the simple comparative adjective 'better' seems almost naive at the end here and you have to

ask, how could she love him better?! The love is seen as eternal and totally idealised.

Did you know?
Elizabeth Barrett Browning's family did not want her to marry Robert so she eloped with him. They both worked as poets - arguably an unusual relationship at the time.

Themes
- Love
- Relationships
- Worship

Prompt Questions
- The poet does not explore any negative consequences of love. Do you think this matters?
- Compare this view of love with that offered in the other sonnet in your collection - *Sonnet 29* by Edna St Vincent Millay. Which do you prefer and why?

Farmhand - James K Baxter

This poem describes a young man who seems socially awkward and unable to connect romantically with the girls he watches at the local dance hall. He is portrayed as diffident and clumsy in this environment but is transformed in the natural world. The farm is his domain; in his element there, he appears confident, strong, graceful, secure and sensitive. Baxter hints to a dark secret - an 'old wound' which is torn open by the music of the dance hall - but this hint of a backstory is never developed, leaving the reader wanting more. The farmhand - who is never named and therefore seems to have no identity beyond his job - has 'awkward hopes' and 'envious dreams', but keeps his story to himself, making him a complex, enigmatic figure.

Form and Structure
Although there is no regular line length to this seemingly conversational poem, it is structured around five end-stopped quatrains which give a formal dignity to the verse. There's a sense that we are meant to take this young man and his situation seriously. More subtly, there is a regular internal half-rhyme in each stanza whereby the second and third lines chime together: *back/joke, flowers/tears* and *side/Instead* are examples of *consonance* whilst *making/breaking* and *strong/song* are full rhymes. It's perhaps worth noting that these full rhymes come as we learn about the farmhand's strength and sensitivity: he is at home on the farm and the full rhyme helps to solidify this positive impression of him while the half-rhymes feel tentative and uncertain, reflecting the way he feels in society.

The repeated use of 'But' in stanzas 2, 3 and 6 creates a sense of the narrator constantly offering new insights into the farmhand, adding layers of complexity to his character as the poem progresses. You could also consider the way the poem is structured so that adjectives are used quite negatively to describe the farmhand in stanzas one to four before his transformation in stanza five (see Language below)

Voice and Tone
There is a conversational tone to this poem with its opening direct address to the reader 'You will see him', the imperative 'watch him' and the exclamatory interjection 'ah' in the last stanza. The perspective is that of a third person narrator who knows there is an 'old wound' and has some knowledge or insight into the 'slow-

growing' mind of the man with 'awkward hopes' and 'envious dreams'.

The tone of the poem is gentle, almost melancholy or sad, although it ends on a beautiful note of warm appreciation.

Language
With a title like *Farmhand* it is perhaps not surprising that images of the natural world feature prominently. It is notable that one of these images is linked to the farmhand himself which helps to create the sense that he is at one with the land. In two powerful *similes,* the girls are 'drifting like flowers' and the crops are as 'slow-growing as his mind'. Here Baxter also manages to contrast flowers and vegetables: the beautiful but essentially cosmetic aspect of nature (flowers) and the less attractive but nutritious and therefore necessary aspect (vegetables). Arguably there is some gendering here as well so that the farmhand's hard-working, unattractive masculinity is contrasted with the beautiful but superficial girls. The idea that there is depth to the farmhand's character is also conveyed in the image of the *slow-growing* crop as opposed to the decorative flower.

There is a powerful metaphorical description of ploughing which is described memorably as 'the earth wave breaking', with the *enjambment* helping to emphasise that picture of the earth turning over in a wave-like motion as the plough moves along.

The final image of the farmhand 'listening like a lover to the song ....of a new tractor engine' is particularly strong. Not only does it celebrate agricultural life with the *metaphor* of a tractor engine singing 'Clear, without fault', but it also reminds us that the farmhand is 'like a lover' in this natural environment even if he can't be a lover in the dance hall. He is in love with the land, with his job.

Adjectives are used throughout the poem to convey aspects of the farmhand: he is 'careless', 'red', 'sunburnt', 'hairy', 'awkward' and 'envious' in the first four stanzas, but the fifth stanza transforms him so he is 'effortless' and 'strong'. This reflects the impact the harvest has on him.

The story of the farmhand's trauma is told briefly through *metaphor* as the music 'tears/Slowly in his mind an old wound open'. The syntax is awkward here (you'd expect something like 'slowly tears open an old wound') and this perhaps reflects the difficulty of the trauma which never has any more detail attached to it. It also shows the poet at work using the beginning and ending of lines to foreground and emphasise key words - *tears, Slowly* and *open.*

The image of the 'secret night' early on in the poem in stanza 1 is perhaps a hint towards the depth and complexity of this character who will not - even by the end of the poem - reveal his secrets to us. Arguably, Baxter is using what's called a *transferred epithet* here - the night is not secret, that label belongs to the young man but it is transferred onto the night as he looks out into the darkness.

Themes
- Humans in the natural world
- Masculinity
- Love and relationships
- Secrecy and isolation
- The past

Baxter's poem *Elegy For My Father's Father* tells the story of a similarly unnamed, enigmatic and closed character whose 'heart had never spoken' in 'eighty years of days'. Taken together, these poems suggest a recurring theme of silent masculinity which Baxter himself arguably denies, of course, by writing such sensitive poetry.

Prompt Questions
- What similarities can you find between *Elegy For My Father's Father* and *Farmhand*?
- What picture of women is created in the poem?

Muliebrity - Sujata Bhatt

Muliebrity is a word which has been used in English since the 16th century to suggest key female characteristics. The better-known and more widely used masculine equivalent is *virility*. *Muliebrity* comes from the Latin word *mulier*, meaning woman and an associated word *mollis*, meaning soft. So softness is implied in this definition of femininity just as strength and power is implied in the word virility. This poem is inviting us to rethink all this, however, with a striking picture of a young woman in a rural setting.

The 'girl' of the poem is collecting cow-dung in rural India where it would be mixed with straw and used as an essential fuel for cooking food. At first glance, her job seems revolting, something which is emphasised by the poet through the repetition of 'cow-dung' - it's almost as if the poet can't believe what she is seeing, or that the smell of cow-dung fills the air so it is impossible to ignore. But the poet describes the girl with real dignity and respect. This is done subtly with reference to the way she 'moved her hands and her waist' as well as the powerful closing image of her 'greatness', 'power' and 'glistening' cheekbones.

Gradually, however, it becomes clear that the poet is determined NOT to present us with a photographic image of this girl. Although she recalls the way the girl moves, Bhatt doesn't describe that to us. In fact, ultimately she is unwilling 'to explain to anyone'. So we are left with this fragment of an experience, a flash of a vision of what it is to be a woman. Being a woman, it seems, is nothing to do with gentleness, it is to do with 'greatness', 'power' and the willingness to take pride in what we do. No matter how low or disgusting or tedious her task, this girl is committed and dedicated; she will sacrifice herself in order to get the fuel to feed her family. The final image of her 'glistening' when she finds a 'particularly promising/mound of dung' is quite striking; she lights up at the sight of cow-dung because this is what she has set out to find.

The poem presents a strong picture of the setting (see Language below) but is perhaps most memorable for the way the poet grapples with the problem the girl poses. Bhatt cannot stop thinking about her - she repeats the opening line 'I have thought so much' twice more and also says twice she is 'unwilling' - to *use* her, to *forget* her or to *explain* her. In the end the poem says quite a lot about the poetic process - the way a poet feels torn between representing a life and exploiting an individual. Bhatt's respect for the girl is shown in the way she does not refine the poem; in this case, it's important for us to look at what she doesn't do as well as what she does. So, for example, she doesn't compare the girl using similes or metaphors. Neither does she finish the poem (see Form and Structure). She leaves us with an unrefined thought and with the image of a girl who represents an essential quality of women which doesn't need explaining.

Form and Structure

This poem is loosely structured to reflect the poet's thought process. A sentence rolls over four lines to create the initial image. The rest of the poem is a largely enjambed, unfinished sentence which breaks off mid-line. The initial line 'I have thought so much' is repeated twice. It appears at the beginning of the second sentence which gives the poem an initial appearance of coherence and order, but subsequently it is injected mid-sentence and any sense of a formal structure is lost. This is all quite deliberate, of course, as the poet wants to convey for us a sense of her thoughts tumbling over one another in contradictory waves. In the end she breaks off, perhaps unable to decide how she should construct this image which she doesn't want to forget or explain or exploit.

The tumbling *olfactory images* (see Language below) in the centre of the poem create a strong sense of the cacophony of smells she encounters and it is these, it seems, which almost overwhelm her. Bhatt uses a *syndetic list* here to emphasise the layering of the 'smells surrounding me separately/and simultaneously'.

Voice and Tone

Written in the first person, this is a very self-conscious poem in that we hear the voice of the poet telling us of her struggle or dilemma about using the girl. Bhatt has said that the poem was based on a memory from her childhood. She refers directly to her own role as a writer when she says she has been unwilling to use the girl 'for a metaphor,/for a nice image' which perhaps suggests she is thinking of the way tourists exploit locals for photographs.

It is a reflective poem with a thoughtful, mildly self-critical, almost frustrated tone. At times it seems the poet is in awe of the girl with her 'greatness', 'power' and 'glistening'. In saying she does not want to 'explain' her, there is a sense that Bhatt would like to keep her thoughts private, so there is a slightly reserved, almost secretive edge to the poem. She offers us a glimpse but then withdraws.

Language
The poem uses a very simple vocabulary, perhaps to reflect the simple rural setting and the very routine nature of the girl's occupation. The adjectives used are deliberately plain - 'wide', 'round', 'wet', 'freshly washed' - so that when it appears towards the end, the verb 'glistening' seems extraordinary, almost flamboyant.

Olfactory images dominate the centre of the poem as noted above (see Form and Structure) - cow-dung, road-dust, canna lilies, monkey breath, dust from crows' wings and freshly-washed clothes. This list also establishes the rural setting very clearly and it's worth noting that much more emphasis is on smell rather than the more usual visual imagery. It seems Bhatt is deliberately not creating the photographic image which smacks of exploitation; instead she is giving us something much more real, if a bit unpleasant!

Themes
- Poetic responsibility
- Women
- Poverty
- Sacrifice

- Do you agree with the picture of womanhood presented in this poem?
- In publishing this poem, do you think Bhatt has exploited the girl, despite saying she did not want to use her?

Plenty - Isobel Dixon

On the surface, the 'plenty' of this poem's title relates to water. The poem tells the story of how the speaker's childhood was characterised by lack of water and how now, as an adult, she has plenty. The poem opens and ends with images of the bathroom - going from the negative depiction of an 'old enamel tub, age-stained and pocked' which was 'never full', to the present where 'bubbles lap my chin' and the 'shower's a hot cascade'. The water poverty is the result of 'drought', leaking dams and 'windmills stalled', but Dixon uses this as a starting point for exploring something quite different. The poem is really about the speaker's mother and the way she coped with five children and a grinding poverty which meant 'each month was weeks too long'. She brings the water and poverty together in the final line of the poem where she refers to the past as those 'lean, dry times'. As Dixon emerges into an adulthood of relative luxury, she grows into a realisation of all that her mother did for her and is able to correct some of the wrong ideas she had in her youth.

In particular, she had the idea that her mother was 'mean' and angry, an idea she makes clear in an extraordinary connection between 'windmills stalled' and her mother's smile which seems strained and lacking in any humour or warmth. The smile is a *motif* in the poem. As a child she sees the lips 'stretched back', 'anchored down', a 'clasp' 'clamped hard'. It is only when they are released from poverty - and perhaps the grind of looking after five children - that the mother's smile is relaxed or 'loosed'. The images used to describe the smile are subtle (see Language, below) and speak of a mother who stoically repressed her feelings and took very seriously her responsibilities as a carer.

So the poem is actually about adults and the sacrifices they make for children who are frequently selfish - they 'Skipped chores', 'swiped biscuits' and broke the rules by putting 'another precious inch' of water into the bathtub. Despite the poverty, however, for the speaker these are happy memories of 'lovely sin', 'secret warmth' and 'co-conspirators'. In contrast, now that she is able to have as many long baths or hot showers as she likes - indulging like a 'sybarite' devoted to luxury - she is isolated, misses her 'scattered sisters' and feels nostalgic for 'those bathroom squabbles'. Perhaps what she is saying in the end is that there was *plenty* of love despite the lack of water and despite the fact her mother had to keep a tight control over everything, absorbing all the strain so that the children could be happy.

Form and Structure
The poem is organised over eight quatrains with varying line lengths. Most are end-stopped, allowing for those that aren't to highlight particular features. For example, the pause indicated with a dash between the second and third stanza allows the words 'of mine' to appear foregrounded, suggesting the poet's recognition of her own self-centredness. By contrast, the *enjambment* between stanzas 3 and 4 foregrounds the extensive nature of the shopping list which is spiralling or 'spilling' out of control. A similar effect is achieved between stanzas 5 and 6 where it is the water that is sinfully flowing.

More obviously the poem is structured around past and present - six stanzas are recounted in past tense, two in present tense.

Voice and Tone
Written in the first person, this is a reflective poem with an appreciative tone. The speaker is almost gleeful in the way she recounts episodes from her childhood and we sense her excitement in words like 'Skipped', 'swiped' and 'running riot'. She is also, however, appreciative of the luxury she now enjoys and this is particularly evident in stanza 7 where she describes the cascade of the hot shower with a long, slow progression of clauses - the water is 'plentiful, to excess, almost, here' - elongating the moment with real pleasure. When she says 'I leave the heating on' we hear the voice of almost smug satisfaction. Or is it guilt? Whichever it is, it is undercut by her final stanza where she returns to the respectful appreciation of her mother and of her childhood. Overall the poem is warm, honest and almost apologetically nostalgic.

Language
This poem is full of subtle *imagery* around flow and restriction. The description of the mother's tight-lipped smile is particularly effective. Initially this is compared to the 'windmills stalled', a *simile* which emphasises the rigid, fixed nature of the smile. Dixon also writes that her lips 'stretched back/and anchored down' which suggests tension but also, through the anchor *metaphor,* a sense of restraint - the mother is anchored to reality, a reality of poverty and limits. The smile is also referred to metaphorically as 'a clasp to keep us all from chaos'. On one level this is a slightly childish image with a clasp or clip suggesting a purse. However, this takes us back to the poverty and the mother's need to keep a tight rein on expenditure. Interestingly, of course, we use the verb *to purse* in connection with lips: if someone purses their lips, they press them

together, often to show displeasure which they won't voice. Dixon cleverly hints at this whilst simultaneously conjuring the child's perspective. Later the mouth is metaphorically referred to as 'a lid clamped hard', again emphasising the rigidity and determination of this stoical woman who refuses to give in to the difficulty of her life and has silenced herself in 'quiet despair'. These are not pleasant images of the mother's smile but they all speak of a control and restraint which is later 'loosed' like the water which can now flow freely and abundantly.

The poem is full of subtle sound effects as well. A slippery *sibilance* is used when Dixon describes the mother's concerns - 'She saw it always, snapping locks and straps,/the spilling: sums and worries, shopping lists' - whilst *consonance* emphasises the laziness of 'lovely sin,/lolling luxuriant'.

Themes
- Poverty and wealth
- Mother-daughter relationships
- Memory
- Growing up/childhood
- Stoicism
- Love

Prompt Questions
- Do you think the narrator feels guilty for misjudging her mother?
- Do you think the description of the bath in stanza 1 is significant?
- In describing herself as a 'sybarite' do you think the narrator is expressing guilt, smug satisfaction or something else?

The Three Fates - **Rosemary Dobson**

The Three Fates are figures from Greek myth - three sisters who spun, measured out and then cut the thread of life for humans. Effectively they represent destiny - deciding how long we will live and how/when we will die.

This poem tells the story of an unnamed protagonist (the central character in a narrative or drama) who calls out to the three sisters when he is drowning, presumably asking for his life to be spared. For some reason, they grant his request and give him immortality. What happens then is a bit like Groundhog Day only instead of a day repeating itself, he has to go through his whole life in reverse before starting all over again.

Dobson is not the only poet to philosophise on the strangeness of time, mortality and the human desire to go on. Initially, her poem presents what could be seen as a comic picture of immortality with colloquial phrases like 'He came up like a cork'. But as it progresses, there is an increasing sadness and pathos about this man's existence. He must write poems 'from the end backwards', brush away 'tears that had not yet fallen' and then watch his loved one 'growing younger' until she isn't born. With no time for reflection 'it began all over'. The final image of 'The reel unrolling towards the river' is slightly ambiguous - it suggests, perhaps hopefully, that he will end up in the river and have the chance to die this time, rather than repeat his request for immortality. Alternatively it might suggest he is tied to this existence: his thread of life will unroll to the river and then roll right back up again to the beginning. This image is a little reminiscent of another myth, that of Sisyphus who was punished for deceit by being made to roll a boulder uphill, only to watch it roll down and repeat the action for ever.

Form and Structure
The poem is written in tercets - three line stanzas. It begins and ends at the river, appropriately creating a circular structure which reflects the way the protagonist is condemned to repeat his life, never getting anywhere. The narrative moves rapidly with a quick succession of verb phrases sketching in the details of the man's reverse life: he 'came up like a cork', 'put on his clothes', 'returned to the house', 'suffered' and so on. Dobson uses a *syndetic list* in the final stanza to create an almost cinematic effect of items being removed rapidly from the picture. The speed of his reverse life is, of course, ironically juxtaposed to the reality of his immortality which stretches on endlessly.

The poem feels like a fable but it is left up to us as readers to decide on the moral, if any. Dobson presents life as a seemingly meaningless sequence of events - poems, tears, love, swinging and birth - 'an instant's pause'. With no real detail about the unnamed protagonist or his lover, we are not encouraged to form an attachment to him. In fact, it is made to seem rather futile, isn't it?

Voice and Tone
The poem has a third person narrator who writes as a largely detached observer, giving us very little emotional insight into the man. The narrator tells us that the man 'suffered' and loved his loved one 'wildly', but beyond that there is no information about the man's emotional state. There is some judgement implied in the early line 'It was a mistake, an aberration' to ask for immortality, but whether that is the narrator's judgement or the man's own view is left unclear.

The tone is very factual which goes with the fast pace of the narrative (see <u>Form and Structure</u> above) and there's a sense readers are being left to draw their own conclusion about the moral of the story.

<u>Language</u>
The comic image of the man bobbing up 'like a cork' is the only piece of *figurative language* in the poem, but there are some ironies in the idea of brushing away 'tears that had not fallen' or the thought of a day which 'regressed towards morning'. The alliterative final line 'The reel unrolling towards the river' highlights the ominous nature of the man's existence.

<u>Themes</u>
- Time
- Mortality

<u>Prompt Questions</u>
- Read *Tithonus* by Tennyson which tells the story of another protagonist who requested immortality from the gods. Is Dobson more positive than Tennyson?
- Do you think the narrator is non-judgemental?

Those Winter Sundays - Robert Hayden

Like *Plenty* by Isobel Dixon, this is a moving poem about childhood memory and the way in which young children frequently misjudge the sacrifices parents make, only realising this as they get older, sometimes too late. The poem tells the simple story of a father who got up early every day to make the fire which would warm up the house for his family (by saying 'Sundays too' the speaker implies all other days started in this way). Nobody thanks him for this, or for any other tasks he completes in his undemonstrative way, like polishing shoes. Right at the end of the poem the speaker realises that as a child he didn't appreciate how much his father acted out of love. As a child he was apathetic towards his father 'Speaking indifferently to him'. Having said that, despite building fires to warm the house, there was clearly no emotional warmth in the building since he writes of 'fearing the chronic angers of that house'. However, this is not something that the poet dwells on; there is no detail about the anger, almost as if that is a private matter and not important now that his concern is to acknowledge, rather belatedly, his father's unspoken, sacrificial love.

Form and Structure

The poem has three stanzas of five, four and five lines. There is no obvious rhyme or rhythm but the poem has very distinctive sound patterning - both *alliteration* and *consonance* hold key ideas together (see Language below). In total there are 14 lines which has led some people to comment that the poem can be considered a sonnet of sorts. Since sonnets are traditionally love poems, the fact that this is slightly awry with its lack of rhyme and regularity seems appropriate - it's a sonnet but it doesn't quite realise it, much as the speaker was blind to the form of love offered by his father.

The poem is structured so that the focus moves from the very literal Winter Sundays of the title and first line to the much more abstract rhetorical question - 'what did I know/of love's austere and lonely offices?' which is arguably a universal consideration: as readers, what do we really know about love and the way it manifests itself?

<u>Voice and Tone</u>
The poem has a first person narrator with frequent use of first person singular pronouns - *my* and *I*. It's possible that it is autobiographical although that isn't a central concern for us. The voice is that of an adult looking back on a powerful, repeated childhood experience. The tone is self-critical, ashamed and guilty. The repetition of the rhetorical question 'What did I know, what did I know..?' is almost despairing but quite ambiguous. It could be seen as bitter regret or a pleading self-justification.

<u>Language</u>
A series of words with a <u>harsh 'k'</u> sound hold together the core ideas of the fire, the wintry weather, the father and the son: *blueblack, cold, cracked, ached, weekday, banked, thanked, wake, cold, breaking, call, chronic*. This *consonance* is more marked than in any other poem in the collection so don't dismiss it. It's a great example of how poetry doesn't need rhyme to have a strong auditory impact.

The poem is also suffused with the cold of those Winter Sundays mentioned in the title. The father turns the cold into heat and we can hear the *onomatopoeia* of 'splintering' as the ice literally cracks as it thaws. Despite having 'driven out the cold', however, the father cannot warm the house emotionally. Instead there is a cold indifference and 'chronic angers'. There is a technique called <u>metonymy</u> at work here in the line 'the chronic angers of that house' whereby 'house' is understood to stand for the people who live in the house. More significant is the choice of the word 'chronic' which means long-term but is also reminiscent of Cronus, a figure in Greek mythology who castrated his father and ate his own children because he was warned they would try to overthrow him. Using the word 'chronic' therefore strengthens the idea of tension in the father-son relationship and the sense that behaviours will be repeated across generations unless something breaks the pattern.

Including the above reference to Greek mythology, there are several subtle references to religion. The mention of Sundays is obvious, and it is worth noting that the speaker's father works on the seventh day, unlike God the Father in the Christian tradition. However, the 'cracked hands' could be a hint towards the pierced hands of Christ who sacrificed himself on the cross. The poem's final word 'offices' can mean practical duties but is often used in a religious context referring to the ritual duties performed by monks or clergymen. Religion is not a dominant theme but it helps to underline the ideas of willing sacrifice, ingratitude and belated appreciation that are so important in the poem.

Themes
- Childhood
- Memory
- Parent-child relationship
- Sacrifice
- Love

Prompt Questions
- What similarities can you see between this poem and *Plenty* by Isobel Dixon?
- Is the speaker reconciled to his father in your opinion?

Mid-Term Break - Seamus Heaney

This is possibly one of the most moving, yet restrained and understated poems you will ever read, touching on ideas of loss, grief and childhood memory. If you haven't already read it, please do that now, because once you know what it is about you can never quite recapture that initial shock which makes the poem so memorable for everyone who encounters it.

Once you've read the poem you'll know that Heaney only gradually reveals what has happened, saving the most poignant detail for last, and that the title is deliberately ambiguous, misleading and cruelly ironic. We'll look at these features in more detail below. It is an autobiographical poem which tells the story of the 14 year old Heaney being called back home from boarding school for the funeral of his four year old brother Christopher who was killed in a car accident - 'the bumper knocked him clear'.

It is not clear at the start whether the first person speaker knows why he has been called home but he describes how he passes several hours 'Counting bells knelling classes to a close' using ominous language that suggests a funeral. When he arrives home he encounters a series of strange and awkward scenes - his father crying which is clearly unusual as 'He had always taken funerals in his stride'; old men shaking his hand; strangers; whispers; his mother 'tearless' and 'angry' clutching his hand. It is not until the end of the fifth stanza that we are told there is a 'corpse', and not until the final line that we learn it is the body of a four year old child. The delayed revelation of the poem's subject accounts for much of its power, but this is not a dramatic revelation. There has been a dawning, creeping realisation emerging from a slightly mysterious start. It's a growing unease which makes the ending unsurprising but still the thing we dread.

Form and Structure

The poem comprises 7 unrhymed tercets and a single line at the end. The lack of rhyme contributes to the very natural, understated feeling of the poem but it also serves as a plain background allowing other elements of sound and rhythm to stand out. For example, the first line of the third stanza is notably rhythmic as the poet describes how 'The baby cooed and laughed and rocked the pram'. The verb triplet and the use of obvious *iambic pentameter* (diDUM diDUM diDUM diDUM diDUM) is appropriately bouncy and jaunty, like a baby's nursery rhyme, which emphasises the baby's normal behaviour in contrast to the surrounding images of grief and the awful awkwardness of the funeral guests. Similarly, the *alliteration* and internal rhyme in the second line - 'Counting bells knelling classes to a close' - creates a strong *auditory image* which is the more powerful because the poem lacks a regular rhyme scheme.

The most notable feature of the structure is, of course, that devastating last line. Isolated, it tells a stark truth with a terrible logic. There's a kind of equation here - 'A four foot box, a foot for every year' - which is cruel and shocking. Isolating the line makes it impactful and also serves to emphasise the isolation of the teenager staring down at his younger brother.

Voice and Tone

The poem is obviously told in the first person, from the perspective of a man remembering a traumatic incident from his early teenage years. Much of the poem's power rests in the way Heaney refrains from romanticising the event. The speaker himself conveys very little emotion and certainly does not comment on his own emotions so that the poem feels very muted and emotionally restrained. We might assume he is bored initially because of the way he counts the bells. Later he says he was 'embarrassed' by the 'old men standing up to shake my hand' - perhaps because they are treating him as an adult. But this is the only direct reference to emotion. Arguably, the tone of the poem is very controlled, almost factual - this is seen in the very precise, factual recall of details such as 'two o'clock', 'ten o'clock', the words spoken by Big Jim Evans and the old men, the mention of 'Snowdrops/And candles' by the bedside and the description of the 'poppy bruise'.

There are two references to the fact he is away at school and when he says 'I saw him/For the first time in six weeks' there is perhaps a slight sense of guilt or, if not that, perhaps regret or even resentment. The fact we can't pin down the feeling is testament to the fact that Heaney presents us with a speaker who won't reveal his emotion: he refuses to make this poem sentimental and mawkish. It is left to us to feel the impact of the younger brother's death in that horrible final line.

Language

The language of the poem is mostly very simple and very literal, which fits well with the idea of a childhood memory. As with the unrhymed tercets, however, this simplicity provides a backdrop against which certain elements stand out. For example, the description of the mother who 'coughed out angry tearless sighs'. As with so much in the poem, this is not a romantic picture of a grieving mother. The verb choice 'coughed' is very clever, conjuring that choking sensation which often accompanies the later stages of crying. Using the adjective 'angry' similarly reflects a second stage of grief - the intense crying happened when the teenage Heaney was still at school, now she is focused on resenting the accident and the driver. In the same way, the description of the dead child 'Wearing a poppy bruise' is a beautiful, tender image. The poppy is, of course, symbolic of death and rememberance but it also creates a clear picture of the injury which somehow seems inadequate. The fact that he is 'Wearing' the poppy also seems wrong because the verb conveys a feeling of choice or style rather than accident. Subtly, therefore, Heaney creates a sense of incongruity as well as beauty, refusing to give us any gory details of the accident. As he says, there were 'No gaudy scars'. These details subtly combine to create the teenager's perspective: reference to 'the bedside' and the only simile in the poem -'as in his cot'- make it clear that the young boy looks as though he is asleep. Even though nothing is said, we sense the speaker's difficulty in accepting the reality of death - something which many readers will understand as a common feeling.

A similar incongruity is achieved through the *juxtaposition* of 'Snowdrops' - suggesting life - 'And candles' - suggesting funerals. Notice the way Heaney breaks the line here - we see the Snowdrops, and only then do we see the candles. Perhaps this is the order he saw them - life, then death; hope, then reality. Interestingly these 'soothed the bedside'. The verb choice here is odd, but so too is the object of the verb. Heaney is suggesting that the snowdrops and candles made the bedside more beautiful, softer, calmer. But they do not soothe or comfort him.

The word 'knelling' refers to the tolling of funeral bells. Combined with the word 'close', this is very foreboding, so early in the poem. The *auditory image* gives the poem an *elegiac* feel.

There are a couple of examples of language being used ambiguously in the poem. The 'Break' of the title is a literal break from school, although hardly the holiday that would normally be expected, but it also relates to the broken life/body of the young child. Big Jim Evans' comment that 'it was a hard blow' is obviously horribly inadequate, but can also be seen to reflect both the family's emotional devastation AND the collision with the car. It seems a typical well-meant comment which has an unfortunate double meaning. A similar awkwardness is seen in the old men's *euphemistic* comment 'sorry for my trouble' - a phrase which is commonly heard at funerals where people cannot bring themselves to use direct language.

Themes
- Grief and loss
- Death
- Childhood memory

Prompt Questions
- How well do you think Heaney has recreated the perspective of his teenage self?
- Does the factual tone make the poem more or less moving for you?

Little Boy Crying - Mervyn Morris

Morris is a celebrated Jamaican poet whose humour and sensitivity come across well in this poem which takes a sympathetic look at a child crying because his father has slapped him. In many ways it is deceptively simple: a moment in time is captured and observed empathetically before the life lesson is emphasised. In miniature, though, what Morris manages to capture is the huge gulf between the perspectives of a three year old child and his father, between the instinctively imaginative world of the child and the fearful, anxious and guilt-ridden world of the adult. It's a story of crime and punishment, of authority and discipline, of tough love and consequences. If only it weren't about playing in the rain......

We don't witness the slap which is not mentioned until the end of the first stanza - 'the quick slap struck' - because Morris wants us to focus on the child's reaction which is described in great detail. Neither are we told until the very last line of the poem what it is that the child did to deserve the punishment. When we are told 'You must not make a plaything of the rain' it is, arguably, something of an anti-climax (it is *bathetic*). In some ways this undermines the whole argument for discipline which is established in stanza 3 where we are told of the father's agony and how he 'longs to lift you, curb your sadness' 'But dare not ruin the lessons you should learn'. Is this really an important lesson? Really? It's possible that there is a contextual or cultural significance but playing in the rain isn't obviously dangerous. Alternatively, of course, it could be interpreted as a metaphor where rain represents tears: in other words, you should not try to manipulate people with your tears. This feels like a much better interpretation - it is certainly more subtle and a much tougher lesson for children (and adults) to learn.

Form and Structure
The poem has three unrhymed stanzas and a single final line which contains the proverbial wisdom of the poem and is separated out for impact. The three stanzas are structured so that we move from an intense focus on the physical impact of the slap (stanza 1) to the child's perspective of the slapper, his father (stanza 2) and finally the reality of how the father feels (stanza 3).

Voice and Tone
This is unusual because it is written in the second person and present tense, something which is emphasised through the repeated use of 'Your' in the first stanza. Doing this enables the

observer poet to show great empathy with the child to whom the poem is addressed. Because the speaker can also understand the perspective of the father, the poetic voice comes across as balanced, wise, reasonable and fair. The voice sounds like that of a wise old person who sees everything.

There is also quite a lot of humour in the poem - particularly in the second stanza where the poet uses the language of fairytales. The speaker is laughing gently at the little boy, but not mocking him.

Language

There is a powerful description of the crying child in which the poet uses interesting language. The child's mouth is 'contorting in brief spite' and his laughter has been 'metamorphosed into howls'. Both these verbs suggest distortion and change, a transformation: the child has become almost animal. He is also 'tight' when he was previously 'relaxed'. Howling wolves and transformations introduce us subtly to the arena of fairytales which is how the child understands the world at the moment.

So in the second stanza there is a much more obvious *lexical field* of fairytales with 'ogre', 'grim giant', 'victim', 'tale', 'chopping clean the tree' and 'deeper pits to trap him in'. The poet captures perfectly the violence of these fairytales which are far from innocent, childish stories and which were originally written for young children as a way of teaching them about the dangers of the world. Ironically, this child sees his father as the villain - the 'ogre' or 'grim giant' - rather than the handsome hero: he hasn't yet learned that lesson either.

The language used in relation to the young child is quite harsh and the speaker does not sugar-coat this. The child has 'spite' and 'hate';

he wants to 'trap' his father or make him tumble to the ground, 'dead'. He's brutal - but has apparently been fed on a diet of brutal tales!

The language used to describe the father is arguably more sympathetic. The slap is described in tight monosyllabic terms with harsh 'k' *consonance* to recreate its impact - 'the quick slap struck'. But after that, the language is much more gentle: the father 'longs to lift' with the soft *alliteration* highlighting his love. He wants to 'piggy-back or bull-fight' - both images of playfulness and loving physical contact. When the speaker says the father 'dare not', the verb choice makes the father sound like the victim of the story: he is a slave to the discipline he feels he has to impose on the child.

Themes
- Paternal love
- Grief
- Discipline and authority

Prompt Questions
- How do you feel about the poem's ending? Is it an anti-climax?
- Is the poet more sympathetic to the father or to the child?
- Is the poet making a comment on the way we use fairytales and discipline to educate children?

Rising Five - Norman Nicholson

This poem is about the way humans tend to look to the future and fail to live in the moment. Although it doesn't tell us directly to live in the moment - unlike all those poems written in the tradition of *carpe diem* (seize the day) - the warning is quite a stark one. The poem shows us the flaw in our approach to life through the example of a child who claims he is 'not four...But rising five'. It is easy to dismiss this child, to laugh at him with his 'toffee-buckled cheeks', his wide eyes, his 'little coils of hair' and the very precise fact of his having been alive 'Fifty-six months or perhaps a week more'. The whole of the first stanza is dedicated to making this child seem cute but annoying and a bit ridiculous. However, this mockery shifts as the poet turns his attention to the natural world. Images of spring are used in stanza 2 to reflect great busyness and it is easy to see this as a *metaphor* for youthful vitality - the vitality and busyness of young adult life. The poem then drifts to show the day turning into night and suddenly the whole of adult life is set out before us in a sequence of stages whereby we are always looking to the next thing rather than pausing to enjoy the present. These ideas are brought together in a final, arguably rather moralising, stanza where the images of nature are woven into a discussion about human carelessness. When he writes that 'The new buds push the old leaves from the bough' the poet is focusing on the rather relentless nature of time, but he immediately turns our attention back to human behaviour: 'We drop our youth behind us....We never see the flower' and so on. The final lines of the poem are quite chilling - 'not living/But rising dead'.

Form and Structure
The poem is unrhymed free verse with three significant stanzas focusing on the child (stanza 1), the natural world (stanza 2) and then a fusion of child/humans/nature (stanza 3). Notice the way it's not just the boy who reappears in the final stanza but also his 'toffee-wrappers'. This is a subtle detail which helps with that fusion of stanzas 1 and 2.

Between these core elements, the poem is set out on the page as a series of scattered fragments. These quite deliberately set up a series of parallel phrases that sum up the poem's message: 'not four/But rising five', 'not May/But rising June', 'not day/But rising night', 'not now/But rising soon' and 'not living/But rising dead'. It's easy to dismiss a child's tendency to want to be older, or to justify the way we are conscious of time passing in nature, but the reality is that if we fail to focus on the present and on living, we might as well be dead. The poem's structure really helps to drive home this message.

Most of the poem is in the past tense since it is an anecdote - a story. The final stanza sees a shift into the present tense, however, since this is where the poet pushes his idea. So it moves from the concrete or physical to the abstract or moral.

Voice and Tone
This poem does have a first person narrator - the person to whom the young boy is speaking in the first stanza. The speaker is, however, fairly inobtrusive - there is no comment on what he/she thinks of the boy, for example. In the final stanza the first person plural is used repeatedly in order to draw the reader in: 'We drop our youth...We never see the flower.....We look for the marriage bed'.

The tone is perhaps slightly mocking to begin with (as noted above). I particularly like the image of the coils of hair that suddenly 'Un-clicked themselves upon his head' - suddenly the child loses his babyish, cherubic curls and gets a grown-up hair style - just like that! Similarly the image of his 'toffee-buckled cheeks' is humorous, demonstrating as it does that he is very definitely still a young child, stuffing himself with sweets.

After that the speaker seems increasingly observant, thoughtful and then almost anxious as he/she gives us a succession of images to try and persuade us that he/she is on to something - the toffee-wrappers, the flowers, the fruit, the bed, the grave. The final line is chilling and quite dramatic.

Language
Starting at the end, 'rising dead' is an ironic *juxtaposition,* a *paradox*. 'Rising' is a rather old-fashioned word meaning becoming or advancing towards. The boy could have said 'I'm nearly five', but that wouldn't have given Nicholson this significant word to play with. 'Rising' has positive, uplifting *connotations* (think of bread rising or the sun rising). It is repeated six times in the poem and starts to sound wrong at the point he speaks of 'rising night'; perhaps because we think of the sun rising in the morning and setting at night, it seems wrong to think of the night rising. It is even more absurd when applied to 'soon' - 'not now/But rising soon' - a grammatically awkward phrase. And then, of course, we arrive at 'rising dead' which is probably heavily anticipated. 'Dead' is a particularly powerful and ominous final word with its heavy 'd' sounds.

The images of the natural world are created using some really interesting language. For example, the poet talks about 'the cells of spring', a rather scientific word choice but one which conjures the idea of growth. He says that these 'Bubbled and doubled; buds unbuttoned' with a profusion of *alliteration* that seems to mirror the busyness of the season. When he writes that 'shoot/And stem shook out the creases from their frills' he is using *personification* of the plants, building on the clothing *metaphor* in the 'buds unbuttoned', and making them sound like showgirls. Describing the tree as 'swilled with green' is a subtle way of giving the tree a kind of freshness and fluidity in its colouring (swilled means rinsed) - as though it has been washed into greenness. All this beautiful *imagery* is designed to force us to focus on the moment - even though it is a scene of change and the next stage can be anticipated, it is richly appreciative of the world's beauty and does give emphasis to the current moment.

Flowers and fruit are quite commonly used as *metaphors* for human life so when the poet talks about the stages of bud, flower, fruit and rot, it is clear he is referring to baby, child, adult, corpse. Arguably more subtle is the reference to 'dust' in the scattered part of the poem; along with 'dissected' this suggests death (*ashes to ashes, dust to dust* is a phrase from the Christian burial service).

Themes
- Time
- Life and death
- Ageing
- Carpe diem

Prompt Questions
- How persuasive is this version of the *carpe diem* argument? For example, does the poet present the current moment attractively enough?
- How would you describe the poet's tone in this poem? Is there a shift?
- In what way is this a humorous poem?

Amends - Adrienne Rich

This is a mysterious poem which combines beautiful imagery of
Nature with, arguably, a slightly sinister edge. On one level the
poem is nothing more than a description of moonlight tracing its
way over land, sea, a quarry, a crop-dusting plane in a hangar and
into the trailers where it finally 'dwells upon the eyelids of the
sleepers'. The moonlight, it seems, has come 'as if to make amends',
with the poem's title finally alluded to in the last word.

To make amends means to compensate or make up for a
wrongdoing. The mystery in the poem is exactly for what the moon
is making amends. Rich was an American poet and the references to
the crop-dusting plane and the trailers may suggest poverty among
farm workers. Is Nature somehow trying to make up for this
injustice by blessing the workers with moonlight and soothing them
while they sleep? The poem doesn't give us any clear answers and
the use of the conditional in 'as if' means that the poet doesn't offer
a definitive view: the moon *looks* like it is making amends.

In the absence of a clear narrative, we should enjoy the *imagery*,
especially the *personification* of the moonlight as it creeps its way
across the landscape (see Language below). However, as always
with contemporary nature poetry, there are hints towards an
environmental theme when the moonlight 'leans' against the man-
made object - 'the hangared fuselage/of the crop-dusting plane' -
which is a more awkward movement than its other actions - laying,
licking, flowing, flicking, pouring, soaking and dwelling. 'Leans'
suggests a slightly slanted action which is not fluid or natural. So
Rich might be making a subtle distinction here, suggesting that
Nature and man-made objects are not in complete harmony.
Despite this, Nature is still sympathetic towards the poor, possibly

exploited workforce. This gives another, deeper, level of meaning to the poem which is supported by the word 'gash' used to describe the wound inflicted by humans on the landscape when constructing the 'sand-and-gravel quarry'.

The poem's opening - 'Nights like this:' - may be an *intertextual* reference to Shakespeare's *Merchant of Venice*. At the beginning of Act 5, the lovers Lorenzo and Jessica (daughter of Shylock, the Merchant of Venice) are sitting outside talking about the moon. Lorenzo says

'The moon shines bright: in such a night as this,
When the sweet wind did gently kiss the trees
And they did make no noise, in such a night
Troilus methinks mounted the Troyan walls
And sigh'd his soul toward the Grecian tents,
Where Cressid lay that night.'

They go on to make a series of statements beginning 'In such a night....', but the focus is firmly on love and love-making. It's all very romantic - as is typical of writing about the moon. If Rich is making an intertextual reference to this moment in the play then she is playing with the connection: her poem is not about love between humans, but love from the natural world towards humans. There's an irony, perhaps, in that the sleepers are not awake appreciating the moon; unlike Lorenzo and Jessica they are not positively connected to other humans. On the other hand, there may be no intertextual reference at all; there are plenty of songs, for example, with the line 'On a night like this' and it's hardly an unusual phrase!

Form and Structure

The poem has four unrhymed free verse *quatrains* and no full stops. Apart from two colons used to introduce scenes in the first stanza, there is minimal punctuation - just a couple of commas. The effect is to create great fluidity with lots of *enjambment* and a set of rolling, continuous actions introduced with the repeated phrase 'as it'. This phrase appears eight times in the poem before it is transformed into the final, significant 'as if' in the last line.

Voice and Tone

The poem has an anonymous third person narrator. It is an observation largely without commentary until the final line which offers an interpretation with 'as if'. There are a couple of slightly judgemental words used however. The description of the moonlight as 'unavailing pours into the gash' suggests two things: first that the moon's action is ineffective, achieving nothing (this is the meaning of unavailing) and second, of course, that human activity has wounded the landscape, as mentioned above, creating a 'gash'.

Language

Anaphoric repetition of the formula 'as it' + verb dominates the poem making it read like a list of actions: *as it picks, rises, licks, flows, flicks, pours, leans, soaks, dwells.* Looking at these verbs in isolation - and setting aside 'leans' (see the discussion above) - reveals an increasing intensity, giving the sense that the moonlight gathers force as it moves across the landscape, almost as if it is in search of the sleepers. To dwell is to stay or to rest.

The moonlight is personified through the verb choices, especially 'licks' and 'laying its cheek', which conveys a gentle, loving character. The fact that the moonlight 'licks the broken ledge' suggests its desire to heal. In literature the moon is often a female symbol (because it has monthly cycles) and some commentators have seen this poem as advancing female qualities of sympathy and nurture.

After the almost harsh, noisy images of the first stanza - the 'cold' apple tree and the star 'exploding out of the bark', Rich uses delicate language with sound-patterning connecting key words like 'picks', 'licks', 'flicks', and *alliteration* connecting 'flows' and 'flicks' or 'trailers tremulous'. This delicate language helps to further characterise the moonlight as gentle and fluid, strengthening this idea of Nature as both powerful and beautiful.

Themes
- Nature
- Compensation

Prompt Questions
- Adrienne Rich is well-known as a feminist writer: do you think her feminist agenda is reflected in this poem?
- Why do you think the moonlight is making amends?

Sonnet 29 - Edna St Vincent Millay

Although the word 'love' does not appear until the eighth line of this 14 line sonnet, this poem is all about love - the end of love, the destructive power of love, the fragility of love - and the seeming impossibility that humans can ever learn from experience that love hurts and doesn't last. The speaker has lost her lover as she says 'And you no longer look with love on me' - a line which makes good use of the line length to show a visual separation between 'you' and 'me', the speaker and her ex.

In the first eight lines - the *octet* - the speaker focuses on the cycle of life, the natural movement of the sun, the moon and the tides. She accepts that these things come and go and says 'Pity me not'. So the sun goes down, fields get brambly and become thickets, the moon wanes and the tide goes out - it's natural. She likens all this to humans when she says she doesn't want to be pitied that 'a man's desire is hushed so soon'. Although she doesn't get directly to love and humans until the seventh and eighth lines, with hindsight we can see her images of the natural world are ambiguous. When she talks about the 'beauties passed away/From field to thicket' she may well be referring to human beauty and the human tendency to thicken with age; when she talks about the ebbing tide we get an image of retreat rather than the ebb and flow; similarly the moon - a frequent symbol of love - is waning (not waxing), so already she is hinting at the fact that love disappears.

At the beginning of the next group of lines - the *sestet* - she is very clear and very negative in the way she speaks about love: it is fragile, ephemeral and destructive. It's like blossom that the wind can attack and blow away and it's like a stormy sea strewing the beach with 'wreckage gathered in the gales'.

It is in the sestet that she brings these things together: in her *mind* she knows love fades, she knows that it's destructive and short-lived, but she asks her ex to pity her because her '*heart* is slow to learn' what her mind knows.

Form and Structure
As stated in its title, this poem is a sonnet. More specifically, it is written in the form of a Shakespearean sonnet with the rhyme scheme ababcdcdefefgg. There is a clear divide between the *octet* - the first eight lines - and the *sestet* - the last six lines. The sestet is

further divided (as suggested by the rhyme scheme) into a *quatrain* (4 lines) and a final rhyming couplet. As with so many of Shakespeare's sonnets, the octet sets up a position which the sestet develops, before the couplet kicks in with a conclusion.

This sonnet is also structured through the repeated imperative 'Pity me not' which features three times in the octet before it is reversed in the couplet to 'Pity me'.

Voice and Tone
The poem has a first person narrator and a direct addressee - 'you' - mentioned on the final line of the octet. The imperatives are obviously directed to the addressee, the ex, but they also work as if she is speaking to us as readers.

There is a shift in her tone between the *octet* and the *sestet*. She begins in a very rational, pragmatic way with her quiet acceptance and her independence in insisting through repetition that the ex 'Pity me not'. It's all very controlled in the first two pairs of lines, but the pace begins to pick up when the third 'Pity me not' is followed by 'Nor' and 'Nor' and 'And' as she develops a string of ideas. The beginning of the sestet offers a pause before she is off again with much more violent *imagery* reflecting a passionate almost anguished, pained mindset - an emotional storm to match the one she describes. Her tone here is much more intense, almost bitter as she is says 'Love is no more/Than ....Than...'. The final couplet is resigned, hurt and almost bitterly self-critical.

Language
Images of the natural world feature quite prominently in the poem as described above. This culminates in a final extended image of the 'great tide that treads the shifting shore/Strewing fresh wreckage

gathered in the gales'. Here the tide is personified through the verb choice 'treads' and is almost seen as a kind of god pacing the shoreline and scattering the wreckage carelessly. Notice that the shore is 'shifting' - the *alliteration* highlights this image of movement and change which is a theme of the poem: nothing is stable or permanent, she seems to be saying. Notice also that 'wreckage' is the only human element in the image: it is a final image of human love which makes this a very poignant and powerful poem. Despite knowing all this, she says she cannot stop her heart becoming a part of this wreckage again.

Themes
- Love
- Time
- Nature
- Ageing
- Grief and loss

Prompt Questions
- Does this sonnet have anything positive to say about love, in your opinion?
- Does it matter if we think this poem is autobiographical or not?

Marrysong - Dennis Scott

This is a fantastic poem for a class debate! It tells the story of a tempestuous woman whose husband cannot quite 'learn' her, despite fantastic efforts on his part. She is portrayed as having dramatic, unpredictable mood swings, plunging from 'the walled anger of her quarried hurt' and 'stones in her voice' to the 'cool water laughing'. She brings him all sorts of grief as the 'shadows of her love shortened or grew'. She is 'constantly strange' and he cannot pin her down. Despite this, they stay together 'Year after year' and the poem ends with him accepting the fact she is unknowable. He is reconciled to the fact that he will always be finding his way with her.

So it's ultimately quite a positive view of marriage - I think - although feminists of both gender will want to challenge the way women are represented in the poem. Marriage is presented as a challenge, an adventure and a journey through highs and lows, ups and downs.

The whole poem is based around an extended *metaphor* of geography whereby the man travels the 'territory' and the 'landscapes of her mind'. When the poet says 'He charted', he means the man drew a map - or tried to. In fact, as soon as he does this 'She made wilderness again' and 'Roads disappeared' so 'The map was never true'. You can't help feeling the woman is messing with him here - is there an implication that she doesn't want to be known? If so, as well as unpredictable and tempestuous, we can describe her as capricious or deliberately awkward. It's not looking good for women!

Some of the language used is quite brutal in the way it portrays the woman. For example, the man is shut out by the 'walled anger of her quarried hurt' which is linked to the later phrase saying there were 'stones in her voice'. The idea of a quarry is something dug deep into the landscape and the poet uses this image to suggest the woman has a deep trauma which she then inflicts on her husband in the form of 'stones' - a vicious tongue-lashing. It's also implied that she makes him cry as the 'Wind brought him rain sometimes, tasting of sea' which must refer to salty tears since rain is freshwater. There's no doubting she's powerful - so much so that she can metaphorically make 'wilderness' and 'change the shape of shores'.

On the other hand, the man is portrayed as persistent ('Year on year'), observant ('under his eye'), forgiving (he doesn't retaliate), thorough and organised ('He charted'), patient ('he accepted') and loyal ('Stayed home'). What a hero!

Form and Structure
The poem has 17 lines and is set out as a dense block of largely unrhymed free verse. With *enjambment* and multiple *caesurae* - frequently mid-line - there is a real stop-start rhythm that is unpredictable and disconcerting - mirroring for the reader the way the man is disconcerted by his unpredictable wife. There are, however, two moments of paired rhyme - *new/grew* and *find/mind* - which perhaps reflect the moments of harmony that occur in the otherwise chaotic marriage.

Voice and Tone
The poem is written in the third person but events are largely seen from the perspective of the man so we can say it is *focalised* through him. The narrator doesn't offer any judgement, really, as he tells the story quite factually. Because of the many short sentences, the poetic voice is quite clipped, detached and almost disinterested - the narrator tells the story but doesn't get involved.

Language
The *lexical field* of geography is crucial to the poem's extended *metaphor* - that a woman is like an uncharted territory. So we have: *territory, seasons, water, stones, charted, wilderness, roads, map,*

wind, rain, sea, shores, hill, country, journey, geography, home, landscape - at least 18 references in 17 lines.

There is also a *lexical field* of time, change and movement: *year after year, seasons, shifted, hour, turning, the day before, disappeared, change, each day new, shortened, grew, constantly strange* - at least 12 references.

These dense *lexical fields* support the poem's main ideas but also serve to create the intensity of the experience the man is describing: his marriage is bewildering as everything comes at him thick and fast. These dense lexical fields recreate that experience for us as readers: the ideas come through in a dizzying daze.

Amongst this dizzying array of images there are some we haven't explored yet:

- a 'territory without seasons' is inherently unpredictable because the seasons offer a structure which allows you to plan.
- 'cool water laughing' is a lovely image which uses *personification* to suggest the rippling sound of cascading water. Water is, of course, essential to life - it refreshes and revives, particularly when it is cool. This is arguably the most positive image of the woman in the poem, starkly contrasted to the anger (normally seen as hot) in the previous line.
- 'Roads disappeared' suggests that all the routes he had plotted disappeared. It's tempting to see this as rehashing old stereotypes of men, women and maps (men use them, women can't read them, that type of thing). In contrast to the organised male map we have the chaotic female 'wilderness'.

- 'the shadows of her love' is an ambiguous image since shadows are normally seen as quite dark and ominous. It's unusual to see shadows and love combined unless to suggest she has cast some kind of darkness over him. Is she a kind of Lady Macbeth?
- 'jaunty helpless journey' brings out a clear sense of the contradiction he feels as 'jaunty' suggests excitement whilst 'helpless' suggests negativity. Again, it brings to mind the cliche of a rollercoaster ride.
- 'constantly strange' is ironic: on the one hand it reflects a truth that she is always strange to him, on the other hand this quality of changing is consistent or constant. It's a joke, I think, although I'm not sure which of them is laughing!

Themes
- Love
- Marriage
- Change
- Men and women

Prompt Questions
- What ideas about men and women emerge from this poem?
- Is this a sexist (mis)representation of women in your opinion?

Not Waving But Drowning - Stevie Smith

Stevie Smith is recorded as saying this poem was based on a story she read once about a man who drowned - his friends thought he was waving to them from the sea but really he was drowning. Her poem takes that literal situation and sees in it the idea that a lot of people pretend to be happy but actually feel 'too far out' - out of their depth and unable to communicate their feelings to others.

On the face of it, this is a simple thing to understand and you may sometimes feel like that yourself. How well do any of us know each other? Fortunately most people do have at least one person they confide in, a person with whom they can be truthful, a person who understands the reality behind a social mask. But the man in the poem says he felt - 'it was too cold always' - which makes the situation Smith describes really tragic.

But also comic - and that's her genius. Using simple language, a lot of repetition and direct speech (even though it's not punctuated), Smith manages to make the situation sound absurd as well as awful. This grim whimsicality is typical of Smith as a poet - her poems are often darkly comic, peculiar and a bit playful. But perhaps she was not 'larking' around, not waving but drowning.....

The poem starts after the main event has occurred: a man has drowned and 'Nobody heard him'. Nevertheless, he continues to speaks from death, 'moaning' that 'I was much further out than you thought/And not waving but drowning'. In stanza 2 we hear the patronising voice of some bystanders who seem to think they knew the man - enough, anyway, to say 'he'd always loved larking'. But they are brutal, cold and heartless in the way they simply add 'And now he's dead'. There is, of course, a stark irony in the fact they blame the cold (presumably cold water) for his death - 'It must have been too cold for him his heart gave way' - when in fact it was their cold-heartedness, their failure to see behind the mask of his 'larking' that contributed to the man's tragedy. This is what he points out in stanza 3 when he is 'Still...moaning'.

Form and Structure

The poem comprises three *quatrains* that are rhymed abcb although the only full rhyme - *dead/said* - occurs in stanza 2. The repeated *moaning/drowning* rhyme from the other two stanzas is really a half rhyme - a sort of missed communication which ties in with the theme of the poem. A similar effect is achieved with the rhythm which always feels as if it is going to happen, and then never quite does. You really need to read the poem aloud to hear this - a lot of the lines come up short or feel awkward.

Structurally, the central comment of the bystanders is framed by two stanzas where there is a lot of repetition (about half the words) and crucially both stanzas end with the words of the poem's title, making it very emphatic and memorable. So memorable, in fact, that for more than 50 years 'not waving but drowning' has been used as a metaphor for people not coping and sending out distress signals which are misread. If we focus on these two stanzas only we see a poem about a sad miscommunication from someone struggling (drowning). It's the insertion of that brutal second stanza which puts the blame on the insincere, patronising, cold-hearted bystanders and makes the poem at the same time darker and more comic. Again, it's really worth reading stanza 2 aloud: create the voice of the bystander and then finish with Smith's narrator saying 'They said'. That line is left deliberately short, creating a pause which communicates both the narrator's disgust and the sense that what was said simply wasn't enough.

Voice and Tone

The poem has a third person narrator and the voices of both the dead man and the bystanders - referred to only as 'They'. Smith doesn't use speech marks to separate out the direct speech, but it's clearly there.

The dead man uses direct address - 'I was much further out than *you* thought' - and this draws in the reader, offering a challenge. His tone in the first stanza is factual but there is a slight shift in the last stanza where he exclaims 'Oh, no no no', with that emphatic repetition suggesting a desperate determination to correct those bystanders and their wrong ideas about him. Switching from 'further out' (stanza 1) to 'too far out' (stanza 2) simultaneously makes him sound more assertive and more despairing.

The bystanders have a glib, shallow, pitying and insincere tone when they say 'Poor chap', a rather patronising, colloquial phrase which gives the man no identity. Using the word 'larking' in the same phrase as 'dead' also seems deeply insensitive.

Language
The poem is very economical with language, using simple and repeated phrases for effect, as noted above. The only adjectives in the poem are 'dead', 'Poor' and 'cold'. There is no description of setting.

The central interest in the poem, though, is the way Smith constructs her *metaphor*: *drowning* is commonly used a metaphor for not coping - when people feel they have too much on, they say they are swamped, drowning, sinking or going under. Less commonly, *waving* is used as a metaphor for communication but it's ambiguous: we wave either to attract attention or as a friendly, happy gesture. Smith's metaphor of 'not waving but drowning' exploits this ambiguity: people see a happy wave, a greeting, when in fact this is a cry for attention.

Themes
- Death
- (Mis)communication
- Despair
- Isolation and loneliness

Prompt Questions
- What do you think Smith is suggesting about society in her poem?
- In what way can this be seen as a comic poem?

She Dwelt Among the Untrodden Ways - William Wordsworth

This is a much older poem than others in your collection. Written in 1798 it is typical of the eighteenth century Romantic poets who wrote with great emotion, drawing inspiration from the natural world. It is also part of a series of five poems about 'Lucy' who died young. It's not clear whether Lucy was a real person but it's thought unlikely: she represents an idealised character type for Wordsworth - a beautiful, natural, unspoiled young woman that he could compare to the rural environment in which he imagined she lived. Imagining her as dead at a young age enables him to explore feelings of grief and loss as well as unrequited love and the isolation that is typical of very rural places.

We don't learn Lucy's name until the final stanza and that helps to give this otherwise unremarkable young woman a bit of mystery. She is introduced using the past tense verb 'dwelt' which signals her death from the outset but more significantly makes an immediate connection between Lucy and her environment. She lives among 'the untrodden ways' suggesting her isolation in an idealised, remote and special, even secret, place. The fact that she is 'Beside the springs of Dove' means that by association she seems fresh, vital, clear and free, like the source water for the River Dove in the Lake District where Wordsworth lived. It's a lonely place that Wordsworth describes; there are few people there to appreciate or love Lucy which creates a sense of sadness. The poem overall has an elegiac quality.

Stanza 2 gives a more figurative picture of Lucy using metaphor and simile. She is a 'violet by a mossy stone' - shy, modest and beautiful - and she is 'Fair as a star' - constantly bringing light and beauty.

Stanza 3 returns to Lucy as isolated and 'unknown' and the sadness intensifies as we are told she 'ceased to be'. Wordsworth really builds up the pathos here by adding - arguably unnecessarily - that 'she is in her grave', in case we hadn't taken her death on board yet. The poem ends with his emotional response - the lamenting 'oh' between *caesurae* which mimics a little catch in the throat or a sigh that escapes from this otherwise very controlled poetic voice. The final line, perhaps surprisingly, introduces the first person narrator - 'The difference to me!'. Some commentators have seen the whole poem as being about Wordsworth but I feel he leaves himself until last so that we have a chance to picture Lucy in her natural environment and can share his sense of loss at the end. Unlike some of his other poems, Wordsworth's emotion doesn't overwhelm this verse, although there are hints of his tendency to exaggeration with the exclamation and the slightly *hyperbolic* star comparison in stanza 2.

Form and Structure
The poem has three quatrains which rhyme abab and have a fairly consistent alternating syllable count (either 8 or 9 followed by 6).

This means the poem feels controlled and somewhat predictable: Wordsworth is using simple rhymes which feel very familiar such as *ways/praise* and *eye/sky*. The simplicity matches the character he is depicting and therefore feels very appropriate.

Structurally the two stanzas about Lucy in her literal environment enclose the more figurative description which mimics the image of the violet 'Half hidden from the eye'. It is subtle details like this which highlight how *crafted* a poem can be, even when it initially seems very short and straightforward.

Voice and Tone
Wordsworth writes in the first person although that is not revealed until the final word of the poem. The tone is sad or melancholy but warm and appreciative. There is a sense of longing and a slight note of self-pity at the end.

Language
The language of the poem is very simple with most of the words being monosyllabic. At the risk of repeating myself, this is done deliberately to reflect the natural simplicity of Lucy, the poem's subject. She is without artifice and the poem is similarly direct. The negative prefix (*un-*) is used twice in the poem as well as in the title, but the impact is not wholly negative is it?' Untrodden' and 'unknown' convey a sense of mystery and privacy.

The *metaphor* of the violet is probably the most striking image in the poem although it is not at all difficult to understand. Violets - particularly wild violets - are intensely coloured, dainty little flowers that grow among thick leaves and are sometimes inconspicuous or 'Half hidden from the eye'. The metaphor 'a shrinking violet' is commonly used to describe someone who is shy and retiring. So

Wordsworth is not alone in seeing violets as modest - a quality he also sees in Lucy. The *simile* 'Fair as a star' again feels a bit cliche. He develops it a little by suggesting she is a unique star, but the essential idea is that she brings light and beauty. These are not complex images, but they are not meant to be ....

Themes
- Love
- Death
- Grief and loss
- Isolation and loneliness

Prompt Questions
- Do you see this as a mournful poem?
- Does Wordsworth convince you about Lucy or are you left wanting to know more? Do you think this is deliberate?

Creative Challenges

Producing your own creative responses to poetry is a great way to get into the themes, ideas and style of the verse. It's possible such work could double up as coursework for your English Language qualification. If not, it will be good practice for the creative work (both fiction and non-fiction) that you have to do in your Language exam. Some of the non-fiction tasks might be the basis for a Spoken Language presentation.

1   *Caged Bird* - Maya Angelou: write the song of the caged bird. What do you long for? What can you see or hear from your cage?
2   *Sonnet 43* - Elizabeth Barrett Browning: write a sonnet of your own in which you construct your own list of 'ways' that you love, admire, despise or hate someone or something.

3   *Farmhand* - James K Baxter: write the story of the farmhand's 'old wound'. What traumatic event in his past is preventing him forming relationships with these girls he watches at the dance? What is the significance of the music that 'tears' at his 'old wound'?

4   *Muliebrity* - Sujata Bhatt: write about this encounter from the perspective of the girl. What does she think of the poet watching her? What is she thinking and feeling about her job of collecting the dung? Does she really glisten when she spots some promising dung? What does it mean to be a woman in rural India?

5   *Plenty* - Isobel Dixon: write a letter to your mother or grandmother describing some things you remember from your early years. Try to recapture the perspective you had as a young child. How did you see your mother? What did you think about the things she stopped you from doing? What about the way she looked? Try to create some interesting images about her face, voice or hands, perhaps, just as Dixon focuses on her mother's lips.

6   *The Three Fates* - Rosemary Dobson: write the birth announcement of a man who has already lived his life. Use the future tense to describe the things that will happen to him, including his death and then reverse back through those key events. Finish with the line 'And then it will begin all over'.

7   *Those Winter Sundays* - Robert Hayden: write a letter to Robert Hayden's father as though you were the poet. Apologise for your ingratitude, explain what you were thinking and tell him how much you now appreciate what he did for you. What experiences of love or adult life have enabled you to show this maturity now?

8   *Mid-Term Break* - Seamus Heaney: write about a traumatic event in the past using first person. Unlike Heaney, allow yourself to explore your feelings. Try to use a wide range of words that pin down precise emotions.

9   *Little Boy Crying* - Mervyn Morris: experiment with writing in the second person present tense. Imagine a situation where someone has been hurt by someone else. Structure your writing like Morris: deal with the physical impact, then the emotional response and finally look at the alternative perspective before finishing with a moral.

10   *Rising Five* - Norman Nicholson: research the way English poets have used the *carpe diem* motif. Prepare a presentation in which you introduce your peers to some of these poems. Compare them with Nicholson's writing. Which do you prefer and why?

11   *Amends* - Adrienne Rich: write a description of sunlight falling on the landscape and entering a particular house. Use different verbs to those chosen by Rich but try to mirror her approach with some personification. Give your sunlight a purpose in settling where it does at the end of your piece.

12   *Sonnet 29* - Edna St Vincent Millay: create a slide presentation of this poem using carefully selected images to represent the different lines. Choose music to accompany the slides. Write a short evaluation of your choice of music.

13   *Marrysong* - Dennis Scott: write a speech arguing for or against the representation of women in this poem. Make the speech to your peers. If someone else will take the counter position you can set up a debate. The motion could be: This house believes Scott's representation of women in *Marrysong* is fair.

14   *Not Waving But Drowning* - Stevie Smith: write a news report which expands on the details of the poem. Use the bystanders' words in quotes from named friends/family of the victim. Create the victim's back story. Include a quote from a psychologist that explores social isolation and the way some people are unable to show their true despair before it is too late.

15   *She Dwelt Among the Untrodden Ways* - William Wordsworth: research the other four 'Lucy' poems and prepare a

presentation for your group. Is there a sequence? Where does your poem fit in the sequence? How are images of the natural world used in the other poems?

Exam-style Questions

1   Explore the way Angelou approaches the idea of freedom in *Caged Bird*.

2   How does Elizabeth Barrett Browning convey powerful ideas about love in *Sonnet 43*?

3   Explore the way Baxter presents the connection between humans and the natural world in *Farmhand*.

4   How does Baxter vividly convey ideas about the central character in *Farmhand*?

5   How does Bhatt convey powerful ideas about what it means to be a woman in *Muliebrity*?

6   How does Dixon vividly convey memories of childhood in *Plenty*.

7   Explore the way the writer presents relationships between parents and children in *Plenty* or *Those Winter Sundays*.

8   Explore the way Dobson approaches ideas about life and death in   *The Three Fates*.

9   How does Hayden powerfully convey feelings of regret in *Those Winter Sundays*?

10   How does Heaney vividly convey ideas about grief and loss in *Mid-Term Break*?

11   Explore the way Morris uses phrases for striking effect in *Little Boy Crying*.

12   How does Nicholson present interesting ideas about ageing in *Rising Five*?

13   How does Rich create a strong sense of mystery in *Amends*?

14   Explore the way Edna St Vincent Millay presents her thoughts about love in *Sonnet 49*.

15   How does Scott create strong ideas about relationships in *Marrysong*?

16   Explore the picture of women created by Scott in *Marrysong*.

17   How does Smith create strong feelings in the reader in *Not Waving But Drowning*?

18   How does Wordsworth powerfully convey the speaker's feelings for Lucy in *She Dwelt Among the Untrodden Ways*?

Assessment Criteria

To do well you will be expected to

- make a perceptive, convincing and personal response
- show a clear understanding of the text and its deeper implications
- respond sensitively and in detail to the way the writer achieves his/her effects
- Integrate a lot of well-selected reference to the text

The Assessment Objectives for this paper are equally weighted.

AO1 Show detailed knowledge of the content of literary texts, supported by reference to the text.

AO2 Undertand the meanings of literary texts and their contexts, and explore texts beyond their surface meanings to show deeper awareness of ideas and attitudes.

AO3 Recognise and appreciate ways in which writers use language, structure and form to create and shape meanings and effects.
AO4 Communicate a sensitive and informed personal response to literary texts.

Exam Hints

- Break down the question – be clear that you will have to address WHAT and HOW (the content AND the way the poem has been written) – the question will often direct you to a theme (eg loss) and focus you on style (eg powerfully presents/vividly creates).
- Plan – make sure your plan has clear points about the topic so that you can show your understanding of the poem's content
- Support all your points with quotation – multiple quotation if possible
- Stylistic and language comment should accompany the quotation
- Explore effects – the impact on the reader or the different interpretations that might be possible
- Create paragraphs that have the following shape:
  POINT – responding to the question focus
  EVIDENCE - quotation with reference to poetic technique
  DISCUSSION – explore effects/interpretation
  Your teacher may have an alternative version of this PED structure – be guided by your teacher.

Glossary

Alliteration: term used to describe a series of words next to or near to each other, which all begin with the same sound. This creates particular sound effects eg *a hairy hand, the luscious leaves*

Allegory: like metaphor – a story told in simplified form but with hidden meaning. The component parts represent something else.

Allusion: a reference – a classical allusion is a reference to a story from Ancient Greece or Rome.

Ambiguity (noun), **ambiguous** (adjective): (from the Latin for 'doubtful, shifting') the capacity of words and sentences to have double, multiple or uncertain meanings. A **pun** is the simplest form of ambiguity, where a single word is used with two sharply different meanings, usually for comic effect. Ambiguity may also arise from **syntax** (when it is difficult to disentangle the grammar of a sentence to resolve a single meaning), and from **tone** (where the reader cannot tell, for example, whether a given text is to be read seriously).

Anaphora: or **anaphoric repetition** - repetition of a sequence of words at the beginning of consecutive lines.

Antithesis: opposite.

Association or **Connotation:** a word can suggest a range of associations and connections in addition to its straightforward dictionary meaning. For example, *heart* has many associations with love, courage and other human values, besides its literal, biological meaning.

Assonance: repetition of identical or similar vowel sounds in neighbouring words. It is distinct from rhyme in that the consonants differ while the vowels match eg *Shark, breathing beneath the sea/Has no belief, commits no treason.*

Asyndetic list: a list without 'and' between items.

Ballad: songlike poems with a strong story.

Bathos: anti-climax. **Bathetic** is the adjective, meaning anti-climactic or disappointing.

Caesura: plural **caesurae** – a pause.

Connotations: associated ideas.

Dialogue: words spoken by two or more people in conversation.

Direct speech: words spoken and shown in speech marks eg He said 'I have been crying' (see Reported speech).

Elegy: formal lament for the dead. **Elegiac** is the adjective.

Emotive language: language that provokes a strong emotional response.

Enjambment: where lines of poetry are not stopped at the end, either by sense or punctuation, and run over into the next line. The completion of the phrase, clause or sentence is held over.

Epigraph: short quotation or saying at the beginning of a poem or story, intended to hint at its meaning.

Euphemism: (from the Greek for 'speaking fair') unpleasant, embarrassing or frightening facts or words can be concealed behind a euphemism: a word or phrase that is less blunt, rude or frightening than a direct naming of the fact or word might be. Hence 'to kick the bucket' is a euphemism for death; 'would you like to wash your hands?' is a polite euphemism for the question 'would you like to urinate?' Sexual functions, death and body parts are typically disguised in this way in common speech.

Exclamative: exclamation.

Figurative language: language which is not literal – it relies on *figures* such as similes and metaphors.

Foregrounding: placing at the front/to the fore.

Free verse: poetry which is unrhymed and without form.

Hyperbole (from the Greek for 'throwing too far') emphasis by exaggeration.

Iambic pentameter: 10 syllable lines organised into five groups of two syllables - one unstressed, one stressed - diDUM diDUM diDUM diDUM diDUM.

Imagery: words used to create a picture or sensation, through **metaphor, simile** or other figurative language. Usually **visual** imagery - something seen in the mind's eye – but also
auditory imagery - represents a sound
olfactory imagery - a smell
gustatory imagery - a taste
tactile imagery - touch, for example hardness, softness, wetness, heat, cold.

In media res: in the middle of things.

Intertextuality: using another text to shape meaning in a new text.

Irony (from the Greek for 'dissembling') irony consists of saying one thing when you mean another. Irony is achieved through understatement, concealment and allusion, rather than by direct statement.

Juxtaposition: two things placed close together with contrasting effect.

Lament: passionate expression of grief or sorrow.

Lexical field: set of words.

Narrator or **Speaker**: one telling the story, the **narrative**.

Metaphor: in metaphor, one thing is compared to another without using the linking words like or as, so it is more direct than a simile. One thing is actually said to be the other eg *My brother is a pig. The man is an ass*. Verbs can also be used metaphorically: *love blossoms*. Metaphors create new ways of looking at familiar objects and are also commonly found in everyday speech eg *the root of the problem*.

Metonymy: the substitution of a part or an attribute for the thing meant, for example a suit could be a metonym for a city worker.

Mimesis: imitation.

Motif: a recurring idea

Narrative: story.

Narrative viewpoint: there are two main narrative viewpoints. In a **first person narrative**, the narrator is a character in the story who retells his or her first hand account of events. In a **third person narrative**, the narrative voice stands outside the story and is not a character. This type of narrative voice tends to be more objective and often is omniscient (that is, all seeing), therefore able to show the reader the thoughts of all the characters.

Onomatopoeia: where words sound like the things they describe eg *hiss, crash, murmur, creak*.

Oxymoron: a figure of speech that combines two contradictory terms eg *bitter sweet, living death, wise fool.*

Pathetic fallacy: the attribution of human feelings and responses to the natural world eg sullen clouds.

Paradox: (from the Greek for 'beside-opinion') an apparently self-contradictory statement, or a statement that seems in conflict with logic or opinion. Lying behind this superficial absurdity, however, is a meaning or a truth.

Perspective: point of view.

Personification: a form of figurative language in which animals, inanimate objects and abstract ideas are addressed or described as if they were human eg *The breeze whispered gently. The trees waved their tops.*

Power words: words that have a powerful effect in a text.

Quatrain: group of four lines.

Refrain: repeated line or lines – like a chorus in a song.

Reported speech: words reportedly spoken, not within speech marks eg *He said that he had been crying.*

Semantic field: group of words which are linked by meaning – see **Lexical field.**

Sestet: group of six lines.

Sibilance: the recurrence of sounds known as sibilants which hiss - s, sh, zh, c, ch – eg *Ships that pass in the night, and speak each other in passing.*

Simile: in a simile, one thing is compared to another using the linking words *like* or *as* eg *as big as a giant; he smoked like a chimney.*

Sonnet: a poem comprising 14 lines of ten syllables with a defined rhyme scheme.

Structural pivot: turning point.

Symbol/symbolism: a symbol is a person, place, or thing that comes to represent an abstract idea or concept - it is anything that stands for something beyond itself. Symbols are often universally understood eg green = jealousy; poppy = remembrance; cross = sacrifice. Linked to **metaphor** but not quite the same – a metaphor is more consciously creative and original.

Syndetic list: list with 'and' between the items.

Transferred epithet: a figure of speech in which an adjective (an epithet or label) is attached to a noun other than the person or thing it is actually describing.

Printed in Great Britain
by Amazon